España, Aparta de mí este Cáliz
Spain, Take This Cup from Me

España,
Aparta de mí este Cáliz

*Spain,
Take This Cup from Me*

by **César** Vallejo

*Translated by Clayton Eshleman
and José Rubia Barcia*

Grove Press, Inc., New York

ISBN: 0-394-49263-3
Grove Press ISBN: 0-8021-0049-x
Library of Congress Catalog Card Number: 73-21046
First Printing
Distributed by Random House, Inc., New York
GROVE PRESS, INC., 53 East 11th Street, New York, New York 10003

Some of these poems in American versions appeared in: *Cater-pillar, The World, Sesheta*. "César Against Vallejo" appeared
in *Parnassus*.

Assistance for the publication of this volume was given by the
Center for Inter-American Relations.

Índice

Contents

César Against Vallejo

Against the Professional Secret
Moscow Against Moscow
Charles Against Chaplin

All unpublished books by César Vallejo, the stock of his unpublished emotion and, as I see it, the key to his being, the thing against itself.

His being, not the philosophy one can extract from his being, but the force that gives character to his poetry, that compelled me in 1962 to begin in earnest to seek to destroy the Against wedged in my own name,

this Against, the cross on which he is nailed and

at the same time, his crux, the point to tap if one seeks the man's poetry.

In 1965 I went to Lima, Peru, feeling that I should complete my translation of his *Human Poems* on his native grounds. What a mistake that was. At best, the ghost of Vallejo in Peru, and the ghost of Peru in Vallejo. A city and a country cured on the spit of repression and death, a body of poetry wrung hollow on repression and death—

yet, as Juan Larrea has pointed out, Vallejo did carry an archetype, as all great poets do, and his archetype was the infantile complex bequeathed to Peru by mother Spain, a colonization without resolution, a complex that seeks to be reabsorbed, that searches out its own disperson, its death. Vallejo's journey was from mother to Mother, Spain was his European center of gravity; it is as if he crawled there to deposit his gold.

In Vallejo the poetry of a scourged country seeks its rapist, to return to the rapist the very life that was defiled, and this return is made as the rapist itself is dying; in this sense is there a mesh, that profound resolution we feel is archetypal,

and to put it this way of course says very little about the personal César who wandered in Europe for fifteen years, making five trips to Spain interspersed with three trips to Russia, all of them from his base that was Paris. He went to Paris, he tells us, "to be a son" yet the French could not really baptize him, or, to put it another way, it was only in the revolutionary crossfire of Spain and Russia that the eternal Peruvian boy, magnetized to the art center of the Western World, was able to *become* a son.

For Vallejo could not simply make an art;

the alchemy of his art could only be realized through seeking out those forces that cared nothing about art, political revolution in short,

that is, his masochism was such that he had to make a commitment to Soviet Communism, and then in the death of its promise conceive his own parody of the Apocalypse,

again an occurrence that is as historical as it is willed,

for the Spanish Civil War *was* the death of "the mother"—there is now in the soul of man the knowledge that no revolution will essentially change things. Vallejo carries this knowledge in his *Spain, Take This Cup from Me* like a virus; he cannot kill and is broken on the act of *your* killing—If we ask why he did not participate with his body in the Republican cause, we have only to consider this hub he was broken upon,

which is the essence of his Christianity, and the point of departure of the present book.

In Vallejo, profoundly in Vallejo, the dyke between the man of culture who smokes his hookah while his ghostly brother murders to replenish his hashish, gives way—

the cultural colonist and his extension, the warrior, cease to be effective, the machine stalls, the absurd wall between the soul and its aggressions in the world that for centuries was viewed simply as the way life is, crumbles,

Vallejo can no longer keep his finger in that absurd wall that has blood on one side and art on the other; he withdraws his finger, so to speak, and the accumulated pressure dissolves the dyke,

which in a personal way is Vallejo's Against,

for the dyke also gave him his being. He was not a pacifist; he knew very well that the enemy of Man never lets its gun fall, on its own accord, to the earth, that the only way the enemy is overcome is through force,

and so deeply was this hook of contradiction twisted in César Vallejo he could never make *use* of it—but he could reveal it as his *Revelations*,

and the stunning irony of *Spain, Take This Cup from Me* is that it takes the hope of a sometime new heaven new earth and cooks it in personal tragedy; *The Gospel of Matthew* and *Revelations* are in *Spain, Take This Cup from Me* like truffles in a pâté—you can see the specks of them, slightly taste their flavor, but they are subsumed, put in the service of another substance. "7" is still magical—but it is a sapped magic, no longer in being, but in metal—the lamb speaks not from the fire of Last Judgment but with its leg tied to an inkwell—

"The illiterate for whom I write"

—in that line Vallejo's passion, his faith that Marx had given a functional identity to the New Testament, is captured. What a moving line, and even more moving are the two lines that end his poem to the illiterate ox-driver Ramón Collar:

"Back here, Ramón Collar, at last, your friend:
Hello there, fellow man, kill & write!"

It is in this Against, this wall that breaks crookedly through Vallejo's being, that we can also sense the end of a certain kind of art,

an art in which source is compelled into being its own subject,

the poem with "subject matter," a poem "on war," for

example, a poem "on love,"—for once the dyke breaks air and water intermingle,

the public and the personal fuse,

A process begins, a flux in contrast to a cross,

and one can feel this birthing in Vallejo, like a louse nibbling, in Vallejo the potential flux is felt as nonsense shutting off common sense, from moment to moment, like a mechanism short-circuiting. In perhaps his single greatest poem, "Spanish Image of Death," a Bruegel-like "la Muerte" passes, throwing into dwarf-relief the landscape of the soul—she moves swiftly, with long skinny legs, with a bobbing neck and crazed gaunt face—to her body, like ammunition-belts and grenades, are strapped Vallejo's reserves; she carries his cognac, his "reality principle"—and I insist the insane force of this poem can only be understood in the metaphor of a wild flow starting to invade a rationalistic obsession with life, "Fuck You, Descartes!" Vallejo yells over his shoulder as he boards the train for Madrid, and the Madrid he journeys to is a field strewn with corpses,

a battlefield between two ramparts; at each end of *Spain, Take This Cup from Me* a rampart—the first being his "Hymn to the Volunteers for the Republic" and the second the title poem that in effect ends the book. Between these two ramparts are the twelve poems of the gored cities of Spain, a network of the dead—at the far end of the rampart of apocalypse-smashed-history is the rampart of the schoolroom, and with what vengeance, where the infantile-complex is scrawled like a cartoon,

a schoolroom that is the world in which we are all children,

from which mother-Vallejo is withdrawing,

This wolf made up like a schoolmarm

holding its finger to its muzzle, shushing us to be quiet as it slips out the door—

Soon you will all be alone, it grins at us, without a cross, without an accumulated history—I am leaving you and taking the "teachings" with me—I am the soul of an old being withdrawing through your being,

and it does leave us, and left alone with our unsharpened

pencils we see the blackboard it has left us with, a blackboard filled with chalky zeros, hundreds of little monads each of us have carefully drawn,
 and then with thunder-clap
 the flood surges through the wall.

—CLAYTON ESHLEMAN
January, 1973

España, Aparta de mí este Cáliz
Spain, Take This Cup from Me

I. Himno a Los Voluntarios
de la República

Voluntario de España, miliciano
de huesos fidedignos, cuando marcha a morir tu corazón,
cuando marcha a matar con su agonía
mundial, no sé verdaderamente
qué hacer, dónde ponerme; corro, escribo, aplaudo,
lloro, atisbo, destrozo, apagan, digo
a mi pecho que acabe, al bien, que venga,
y quiero desgraciarme;
descúbrome la frente impersonal hasta tocar
el vaso de la sangre, me detengo,
detienen mi tamaño esas famosas caídas de arquitecto
con las que se honra el animal que me honra;
refluyen mis instintos a sus sogas,
humea ante mi tumba la alegría
y, otra vez, sin saber qué hacer, sin nada, déjame,

desde mi piedra en blanco, déjame,
solo,
cuadrumano, más acá, mucho más lejos,
al no caber entre mis manos tu largo rato extático,
quiebro contra tu rapidez de doble filo
mi pequeñez en traje de grandeza!

Un día, diurno, claro, atento, fértil
¡oh bienio, el de los lóbregos semestres suplicantes,
por el que iba la pólvora mordiéndose los codos!

Hymn to The Volunteers
for the Republic

Spanish volunteer, civilian-fighter
with veritable bones, when your heart marches to die,
when it marches to kill with its world-wide
agony, I don't know truly
what to do, where to place myself; I run, write, applaud,
cry, glimpse, shatter, they put out the light, I tell
my chest to end, good, to come,
& I want to degrace myself;
I uncover my impersonal forehead until I touch
the vessel of blood, I stop,
my stature is stopped by those famous falls of the architect
with those with which the animal honors itself that honors me;
my instincts flow back to their ropes,
happiness smokes before my tomb
&, again, without knowing what to do, without anything, leave
me,
from my blank stone, leave me,
alone,
quadrumane, closer, much more distant,
since your long ecstatic instant won't fit between my hands
I swirl my tininess, costumed in greatness,
against your double-edged speed!

One fertile, attentive, clear, diurnal day
oh biennial, those black semesters of begging,
through which the gunpowder went biting its elbows!

¡Oh dura pena y más duros pedernales!
¡Oh frenos los tascados por el pueblo!
Un día prendió el pueblo su fósforo cautivo, oró de cólera
y soberanamente pleno, circular,
cerró su natalicio con manos electivas;
arrastraban candado ya los déspotas
y en el candado, sus bacterias muertas . . .

¿Batallas? ¡No! ¡Pasionès! Y pasiones precedidas
de dolores con rejas de esperanzas,
¡de dolores de pueblo con esperanzas de hombres!
¡Muerte y pasión de paz, las populares!
¡Muerte pasión guerreras entre olivos, entendámosnos!
Tal en tu aliento cambian de agujas atmosféricas los vientos
y de llave las tumbas en tu pecho,
tu frontal elevándose a primera potencia de martirio.
El mundo exclama: "¡Cosas de españoles!" Y es verdad. Con-
                                            sideremos,
durante una balanza, a quema ropa,
a Calderón, dormido sobre la cola de un anfibio muerto,
o a Cervantes, diciendo: "Mi reino es de este mundo, pero
también del otro" : ¡punta y filo en dos papeles!
Contemplemos a Goya, de hinojos y rezando ante un espejo,
a Coll, el paladín en cuyo asalto cartesiano
tuvo un sudor de nube el paso llano,
o a Quevedo, ese abuelo instantáneo de los dinamiteros,
o a Cajal, devorado por su pequeño infinito, o todavía
a Teresa, mujer, que muere porque no muere,
o a Lina Odena, en pugna en más de un punto con Teresa . . .
(Todo acto o voz genial viene del pueblo
y va hacia él, de frente o transmitidos
por incesantes briznas, por el humo rosado
de amargas contraseñas sin fortuna.)

O hard sorrow & harder flint!
O bridle bits champed by the people!
One day the people struck their captive match, prayed with
anger

& supremely full, circular,
closed their birthday with elective hands;
the despots were already dragging padlock
& in the padlock, their dead bacteria . . .

Battles? No! Passions! And passions preceded
by sorrow with bars of hope,
by the sorrow of common people with hopes of men!
Death & passion for peace, of common people!
Death & passion for war among olive trees, don't misinterpret
it!

Thus in your breath the winds change atmospheric needles
& the tombs change key in your chest,
your frontal rising to the first power of martyrdom.
The world exclaims: "Only the Spaniards!" And it's true.
Consider,

in a balance, point-blank,
Calderón, asleep on the tail of a dead amphibian,
or Cervantes, saying: "My kingdom is of this world, but
also of the other" : point & edge in two roles!
Contemplate Goya, on his knees & praying before a mirror,
Coll, the palatine in whose cartesian assault
a slow walk had the sweat of a cloud,
or Quevedo, that instantaneous grandfather of the dynamiters,
or Cajal, devoured by his little infinite or, even
Teresa, a woman, dying because she wasn't dying,
or Lina Odena, in conflict on more than one point with
Teresa . . .

(Every act or brilliant voice comes from common people
& goes toward them, directly or conveyed
by incessant filaments, by the rosy smoke
of bitter watchwords which failed.)

Así tu criatura, miliciano, así tu exangüe criatura,
agitada por una piedra inmóvil,
se sacrifica, apártase,
decae para arriba y por su llama incombustible sube,
sube hasta los débiles,
distribuyendo españas a los toros,
toros a las palomas . . .

Proletario que mueres de universo, ¡en qué frenética armonía
acabará tu grandeza, tu miseria, tu vorágine impelente,
tu violencia metódica, tu caos teórico y práctico, tu gana
dantesca, españolísima, de amar, aunque sea a traición, a tu
                                                           enemigo!
Liberador ceñido de grilletes,
sin cuyo esfuerzo hasta hoy continuaría sin asas la extensión,
vagarían acéfalos los clavos,
antiguo, lento, colorado, el día,
¡nuestros amados cascos, insepultos!
Campesino caído con tu verde follaje por el hombre,
con la inflexión social de tu meñique,
con tu buey que se queda, con tu física,
también con tu palabra atada a un palo
y tu cielo arrendado
y con la arcilla inserta en tu cansancio
y la que estaba en tu uña, caminando!
Constructores
agrícolas, civiles y guerreros,
de la activa, hormigueante eternidad: estaba escrito
que vosotros haríais la luz entornando
con la muerte vuestros ojos;
que, a la caída cruel de vuestras bocas,
vendrá en siete bandejas la abundancia, todo
en el mundo será de oro súbito

Thus your creature, civilian-fighter, thus your worn-out creature,
stirred by a motionless stone,
sacrifices itself, stands apart,
decays upward & through its incombustible flame rises,
rises to the weak,
distributing spains to the bulls,
bulls to the doves . . .

Proletarian who dies of universe, in what frantic harmony
your grandeur will end, your extreme poverty, your impelling
whirlpool,
your methodical violence, your theoretical & practical chaos,
your Dantesque
wish, so very Spanish, to love, even treacherously, your enemy!

Liberator wrapped in shackles,
without whose labor extension would still be without handles,
the nails would wander headless,
the day, ancient, slow, reddish,
our beloved helmets, unburied!
Peasant fallen with your green foliage for man,
with the social inflection of your little finger,
with your ox that stays, with your physics,
also with your word tied to a stick
& your rented sky
& with the clay inserted in your tiredness
& with that in your fingernail, walking!
Agricultural
builders, civilian & military,
of the active, ant-swarming eternity: it was written
that you will create the light, half-closing
your eyes in death;
that, at the cruel fall of your mouths,
abundance will come on seven platters, everything
in the world will be of sudden gold

y el oro,
fabulosos mendigos de vuestra propia secreción de sangre,
y el oro mismo será entonces de oro!

Se amarán todos los hombres
y comerán tomados de las puntas de vuestros pañuelos tristes
y beberán en nombre
de vuestras gargantas infaustas!
Descansarán andando al pie de esta carrera,
sollozarán pensando en vuestras órbitas, venturosos
serán y al son
de vuestro atroz retorno, florecido, innato,
ajustarán mañana sus quehaceres, sus figuras soñadas y cantadas!

Unos mismos zapatos irán bien al que asciende
sin vías a su cuerpo
y al que baja hasta la forma de su alma!
Entrelazándose hablarán los mudos, los tullidos andarán!
Verán, ya de regreso, los ciegos
y palpitando escucharán los sordos!
Sabrán los ignorantes, ignorarán los sabios!
Serán dados los besos que no pudísteis dar!
Sólo la muerte morirá! La hormiga
traerá pedacitos de pan al elefante encadenado
a su brutal delicadeza; volverán
los niños abortados a nacer perfectos, espaciales
y trabajarán todos los hombres,
engendrarán todos los hombres
comprenderán todos los hombres!

Obrero, salvador, redentor nuestro,
¡perdónanos, hermano, nuestras deudas!
Como dice un tambor al redoblar, en sus adagios:
¡qué jamás tan efímero, tu espalda!

& the gold,
fabulous beggars for your own secretion of blood,
& the gold itself will then be made of gold!

All men will love each other
& they will eat holding the ends of your sad handkerchiefs
& they will drink in the name
of your ill-fated throats!
They will rest walking at the foot of this track,
they will sob thinking about your orbits, fortunate
they will be & to the sound
of your atrocious, burgeoned, inborn return,
tomorrow they will adjust their chores, the figures they've
dreamt & sung!

The same shoes will fit whoever climbs
without trails to his body
& whoever descends to the form of his soul!
Entwining one another the mutes will speak, the paralyzed will
walk!

The blind, upon coming back, will see
& throbbing the deaf will hear!
The ignorant will be wise, the wise will be ignorant!
Kisses will be given that you could not give!
Only death will die! The ant
will bring little pieces of bread to the elephant chained
to his brutal gentleness; the aborted children
will be born again perfect, spacial,
& all men will work,
all men will beget,
all men will understand!

Worker, savior, our redeemer,
forgive us, brother, our debts!
As a drum says rolling, in its proverbs:
"What an ephemeral never, your back!

¡qué siempre tan cambiante, tu perfil!

Voluntario italiano, entre cuyos animales de batalla
un león abisinio va cojeando!
Voluntario soviético, marchando a la cabeza de tu pecho universal!
Voluntarios del sur, del norte, del oriente
y tú, el occidental, cerrando el canto fúnebre del alba!
Soldado conocido, cuyo nombre desfila en el sonido de un
abrazo!
Combatiente que le tierra criara, armándote
de polvo,
calzándote de imanes positivos,
vigentes tus creencias personales,
distinto de carácter, íntima tu férula,
el cutis immediato,
andándote tu idioma por los hombros
y el alma coronada de guijarros!
Voluntario fajado de tu zona fría,
templada o tórrida,
héroes a la redonda,
víctima en columna de vencedores:
en España, en Madrid, están llamando
a matar, voluntarios de la vida!

Porque en España matan, otros matan
al niño, a su juguete que se para,
a la madre Rosenda esplendorosa,
al viejo Adán que hablaba en alta voz con su caballo
y al perro que dormía en la escalera.
Matan al libro, tiran a sus verbos auxiliares,
a su indefensa página primera!
Matan el caso exacto de la estatua,
al sabio, a su bastón, a su colega,
al barbero de al lado—me cortó posiblemente,
pero buen hombre y, luego, infortunado;

What a changing always, your profile!"

Italian volunteer, among whose animals of battle
an Abyssinian lion is limping!
Soviet volunteer, marching at the head of your universal chest!

Volunteers from the South, from the North, from the Orient
& you, the Westerner, closing the funereal song of the dawn!
Known soldier, whose name parades in the sound of an em-
                                                    brace!
Fighter that the land had raised, arming you
with dust,
shoeing you with positive magnets,
your personal beliefs in force,
different in character, your ferule intimate,
your skin immediate,
your language on your shoulders
& your soul crowned with pebbles!
Volunteer girdled by your cold
temperate or torrid zone,
heroes all around,
victim in a column of conquerors:
in Spain, in Madrid, the command
is to kill, volunteers who fight for life!

Because they kill in Spain, others kill
the child, his toy that stops moving,
radiant mother Rosenda,
old Adam who talked out loud with his horse,
& the dog that slept on the stairs.
They kill the book, they fire at its auxiliary verbs,
at its defenseless first page!
They kill the exact case of the statue,
the sage, his cane, his colleague,
the barber next door—maybe he cut me,
but a good man &, besides, unfortunate;

al mendigo que ayer cantaba enfrente,
a la enfermera que hoy pasó llorando,
al sacerdote a cuestas con la altura tenaz de sus rodillas . . .

Voluntarios,
por la vida, por los buenos ¡matad
a la muerte, matad a los malos!
Hacedlo por la libertad de todos,
del explotado y del explotador,
por la paz indolora—la sospecho
cuando duermo al pie de mi frente
y más cuando circulo dando voces
y hacedlo, voy diciendo,
por el analfabeto a quien escribo,
por el genio descalzo y su cordero,
por los camaradas caídos,
sus cenizas abrazadas al cadáver de un camino!

Para que vosotros,
voluntarios de España y del mundo, viniérais,
soñé que era yo bueno, y era para ver
vuestra sangre, voluntarios . . .
De esto hace mucho pecho, muchas ansias,
muchos camellos en edad de orar.
Marcha hoy de vuestra parte el bien ardiendo,
os siguen con cariño los reptiles de pestaña inmanente
y, a dos pasos, a uno,
la dirección del agua que corre a ver su límite antes que arda.

the beggar who yesterday was singing across the street,
the nurse who today passed by crying,
the priest burdened with the stubborn highness of his knees . . .

Volunteers,
for life, for the good ones, kill
death, kill the bad ones!
Do it for the freedom of everyone,
of the exploited & of the exploiter,
for a peace without pain—I glimpse it
when I sleep at the foot of my forehead
& even more when I travel around shouting—
& do it, I keep saying,
for the illiterate to whom I write,
for the barefoot genius & his lamb,
for the fallen comrades,
their ashes hugging the corpse of a road!

That you,
volunteers for Spain & for the world, would come,
I dreamed that I was good, & it was to see
your blood, volunteers . . .
Since then there's been much chest, much anxiety,
many camels at the age of prayer.
The good in flames marches today in your name,
reptiles with immanent eyelashes follow you tenderly
&, two steps away, one step away,
the direction of the water that runs to see its limit before
                                                        burning.

II.

Hombre de Estremadura,
oigo bajo tu pie el humo del lobo,
el humo de la especie,
el humo del niño,
el humo solitario de dos trigos,
el humo de Ginebra, el humo de Roma, el humo de Berlin
y el de París y el humo de tu apéndice penoso
y el humo que, al fin, sale del futuro.
¡Oh vida! ¡Oh tierra! ¡Oh España!
¡Onzas de sangre,
metros de sangre, líquidos de sangre,
sangre a caballo, a pie, mural, sin diámetro,
sangre de cuatro en cuatro, sangre de agua
y sangre muerta de la sangre viva!

Estremeño, oh no ser aún ese hombre
por el que te mató la vida y te parió la muerte
y quedarse tan solo a verte así, desde este lobo,
cómo sigues arando en nuestros pechos!
¡Estremeño, conoces
el secreto en dos voces, popular y táctil,
del cereal: ¡que nada vale tanto
una gran raíz en trance de otra!
Estremeño acodado, representando al alma en su retiro,
acodado a mirar
el caber de una vida en una muerte!

II.

Man from Estremadura,
under your foot I hear the smoke of the wolf,
the smoke of the species,
the smoke of the child,
the solitary smoke of two wheat-ears,
the smoke of Geneva, the smoke of Rome, the smoke of Berlin
& that of Paris, the smoke of your painful appendix
& the smoke that, finally, comes from the future.
O life! O earth! O Spain!
Ounces of blood,
meters of blood, liquids of blood,
blood on horseback, on foot, mural, without diameter,
blood four abreast, watery blood
& dead blood in the living blood!

Estremanian, O not to be yet that man
for whom life killed you & death gave birth to you
& to remain only to see you like this, from this wolf,
how you keep plowing in our chests!
Estremanian, you know
the secret in both voices, the popular & the tactile,
of the cereal! That nothing is worth as much
a big root at the point of another!
Estremanian on your elbows, representing the soul in its retreat,
on your elbows to look at
the fitting of a life in a death!

¡Estremeño, y no haber tierra que hubiere
el peso de tu arado, ni más mundo
que el color de tu yugo entre dos épocas; no haber
el orden de tus póstumos ganados!
¡Estremeño, dejásteme
verte desde este lobo, padecer,
pelear por todos y pelear
para que el individuo sea un hombre,
para que los señores sean hombres,
para que todo el mundo sea un hombre, y para
que hasta los animales sean hombres,
el caballo, un hombre,
el reptil, un hombre,
el buitre, un hombre honesto,
la mosca, un hombre, y el olivo, un hombre
y hasta el ribazo, un hombre
y el mismo cielo, todo un hombrecito!

Estremanian, & not to have land that would have
the weight of your plow, nor more world
than the color of your yoke between two epochs; not to have
the order of your posthumous herds!
Estremanian, you allowed me
to see you from this wolf, to endure,
to fight for everyone & to fight
so that the individual can become a man,
so that masters can become men,
so that everyone can become a man, & so
that even animals can become men,
the horse, a man,
the reptile, a man,
the vulture, an honest man,
the fly, a man, & the olive tree a man
& even the riverbank, a man
& the very sky, a whole little man!

Luego, retrocediendo desde Talavera,
en grupos de a uno, armados de hambre, en masas de a uno,
armados de pecho hasta la frente,
sin aviones, sin guerra, sin rencor,
el perder a la espalda
y el ganar
más abajo del plomo, heridos mortalmente de honor,
locos de polvo, el brazo a pie,
amando por las malas,
ganando en español toda la tierra,
retroceder aún, y no saber
dónde poner su España,
dónde ocultar su beso de orbe,
dónde plantar su olivo de bolsillo!

Then, retreating from Talavera,
in groups of one, armed with hunger, in masses of one,
armed with chest up to the forehead,
without planes, without war, without rancor,
the loss behind
& the gain
lower than the lead, mortally wounded by honor,
crazed by dust, the arm on foot,
loving unwillingly,
conquering the whole earth in a Spanish way,
to retreat still, & not to know
where to put their Spain,
where to hide their orbital kiss,
where to plant their pocket-size olive tree!

Mas desde aquí, más tarde,
desde el punto de vista de esta tierra,
desde el duelo al que fluye el bien satánico,
se ve la gran batalla de Guernica.
¡Lid a priori, fuera de la cuenta,
lid en paz, lid de las almas débiles
contra los cuerpos débiles, lid en que el niño pega,
sin que le diga nadie que pegara,
bajo su atroz diptongo
y bajo su habilísimo pañal,
y en que la madre pega con su grito, con el dorso de una lágrima
y en que el enfermo pega con su mal, con su pastilla y su hijo
y en que el anciano pega
con sus canas, sus siglos y su palo
y en que pega el presbítero con dios!
Tácitos defensores de Guernica,
¡oh débiles,
oh suaves ofendidos,
que os eleváis, crecéis y llenáis de poderosos débiles el mundo!

But from here, later,
from the viewpoint of this land,
from the sorrow to which the satanic good flows,
the great battle of Guernica can be seen.
An a priori combat, unforeseen,
combat in peace, combat of weak souls,
against weak bodies, combat in which the child strikes,
without anyone telling him to strike,
beneath his atrocious dipthong
& beneath his very clever diaper,
& in which a mother strikes with her scream, with the backside
                                                        of a tear,
& in which the sick man strikes with his disease, with his pill &
                                                        his son,
& in which the old man strikes
with his white hair, his centuries & his stick
& in which the priest strikes with God!
Silent defenders of Guernica!
oh weaks ones, oh offended gentle ones,
who rise up, grow up, & fill up the world with powerful weak
                                                        ones!

En Madrid, en Bilbao, en Santander,
los cementerios fueron bombardeados,
y los muertos inmortales,
de vigilantes huesos y hombro eterno, de las tumbas,
los muertos inmortales, de sentir, de ver, de oír
tan bajo el mal, tan muertos a los viles agresores,
reanudaron entonces sus penas inconclusas,
acabaron de llorar, acabaron
de esperar, acabaron
de sufrir, acabaron de vivir,
acabaron, en fin, de ser mortales!

Y la pólvora fué, de pronto, nada
cruzándose los signos y los sellos,
y a la explosión salióle al paso un paso,
y al vuelo a cuatro patas, otro paso
y al cielo apocalíptico, otro paso
y a los siete metales, la unidad,
sencilla, justa, colectiva, eterna.

In Madrid, in Bilbao, in Santander,
the cemeteries were bombed,
& the immortal dead,
with vigilant bones & eternal shoulder, from their tombs,
the immortal dead, upon feeling, upon seeing, upon hearing
how low the evil, how dead the miserable aggressors,
resumed their unconcluded suffering,
finished crying, finished
hoping, finished
aching, finished living,
finished, finally, being mortal!

And the gunpowder was suddenly nothing,
signs & seals crossing each other,
& before the explosion a step appeared
& before the flight on all fours, another step
& before the apocalyptic sky, another step
& before the seven metals, the unity—
simple, just, collective, eternal.

¡Málaga sin padre ni madre,
ni piedrecilla, ni horno, ni perro blanco!
¡Málaga sin defensa, donde nació mi muerte dando pasos
y murió de pasión mi nacimiento!
¡Málaga caminando tras de tus pies, en éxodo,
bajo el mal, bajo la cobardía, bajo la historia cóncava, indecible,
con la yema en tu mano: ¡tierra orgánica!
y la clara en la punta del cabello: ¡todo el caos!
¡Málaga huyendo
de padre a padre, familiar, de tu hijo a tu hijo,
a lo largo del mar que huye del mar,
a través del metal que huye del plomo,
al ras del suelo que huye de la tierra
y a las órdenes ¡ay!
de la profundidad que te quería!
¡Málaga a golpes, a fatídico coágulo, a bandidos, a infiernazos,
a cielazos,
andando sobre duro vino, en multitud,
sobre la espuma lila, de uno en uno,
sobre huracán estático y más lila,
y al compás de las cuatro órbitas que aman
y de las dos costillas que se matan!
¡Málaga de mi sangre diminuta
y mi coloración a gran distancia,
la vida sigue con tambor a tus honores alazanes,
con cohetes, a tus niños eternos
y con silencio a tu último tambor,
con nada, a tu alma,
y con más nada, a tu esternón genial!
¡Málaga, no te vayas con tu nombre!
¡Que si te vas,
te vas
toda, hacia ti, infinitamente toda en su total,
concorde con tu tamaño fijo en que me aloco,

Málaga without father nor mother,
nor pebble, nor oven, nor white dog!
Málaga defenseless, where my death was born walking
& my birth died of passion!
Málaga walking behind your feet, in exodus,
under evil, under cowardice, under the concave unutterable
history

with the yolk in your hand: organic earth!
& the white in your hair tips: the whole chaos!
Málaga fleeing
from father to father, familiar, from your son to your son,
along the sea which flees from the sea,
through the metal which flees from the lead,
level with the ground which flees from the dirt
& to the orders, my God!
of the profundity that used to love you!
Málaga under blows, under mortal coagulation, bandit infested,
hellstruck,
heavenslashed,
multitudes walking over hard wine,
one by one, over the lilac scum,
over an even more lilac & static hurricane,
& to the rhythm of the four orbits that love
& of the two ribs that kill each other!
Málaga of my minute blood
& my coloration at a great distance,
life follows with a drum your sorrel-draped honors,
with rockets, your eternal children,
& with silence, your last drum,
with nothing, your soul,
& with more nothing, your brilliant breastbone!
Málaga, don't go away with your name!
For if you go,
you go
wholly, toward yourself, infinitely whole in its whole,
equal to your fixed size which maddens me,

con tu suela feraz y su agujero
y tu navaja antigua atada a tu hoz enferma
y tu madero atado a un martillo!
¡Málaga literal y malagueña,
huyendo a Egipto, puesto que estás clavada,
alargando en sufrimiento idéntico tu danza,
resolviendo en ti el volumen de la esfera,
perdiendo tu botijo, tus cánticos, huyendo
con tu España exterior y tu orbe innato!
¡Málaga por derecho propio
y en el jardín biológico, más Málaga!
¡Málaga en virtud
del camino, en atención al lobo que te sigue
y en razón del lobezno que te espera!
¡Málaga, que estoy llorando!
¡Málaga, que lloro y lloro!

with your fertile shoe-sole & its hole
& your old knife tied to your diseased sickle
& your post tied to a hammer!
Literal & Malagueñan Málaga,
fleeing to Egypt, since you are nailed
prolonging in identical suffering your dance,
resolving in yourself the volume of the sphere,
losing your water-jug, your canticles, fleeing
with your exterior Spain & your inborn world!
Málaga by its own right
& in the biological garden, more Málaga!
Málaga by virtue
of the road, in view of the wolf that follows you
& because of the wolf-cub that awaits you!
Málaga, how I am crying!
Málaga, how I cry & cry!

III.

Solía escribir con su dedo grande en el aire:
"¡Viban los compañeros! Pedro Rojas",
de Miranda de Ebro, padre y hombre,
marido y hombre, ferroviario y hombre,
padre y más hombre, Pedro y sus dos muertes.

Papel de viento, lo han matado: ¡pasa!
Pluma de carne, lo han matado: ¡pasa!
"¡Abisa a todos los compañeros pronto!"

Palo en el que han colgado su madero,
lo han matado:
¡lo han matado al pie de su dedo grande!
¡Han matado, a la vez, a Pedro, a Rojas!

¡Viban los compañeros
a la cabecera de su aire escrito!
¡Viban con esta b del buitre en las entrañas
de Pedro
y de Rojas, del héroe y del mártir!

Registrándole, muerto, sorprendiéronle
en su cuerpo un gran cuerpo, para
el alma del mundo,
y en la chaqueta una cuchara muerta.

III.

He used to write with his big finger in the air:
"Long live all combanions! Pedro Rojas,"
from Miranda de Ebro, father & man,
husband & man, railroad-worker & man,
father & more man, Pedro & his two deaths.

Wind paper, he was killed: pass on!
Flesh pen, he was killed: pass on!
"Advise all our combanions quick!"

Stick on which they've hanged his post,
he was killed;
he was killed at the foot of his big finger!
They've killed, in one blow, Pedro & Rojas!

Long live all combanions
at the head of his written air!
Let them live with this buzzard b in Pedro's
& Rojas'
—the hero & the martyr's—guts!

Searching him, dead, they surprised
in his body a greater body for
the soul of the world,
& in his jacket a dead spoon.

Pedro también solía comer
entre las criaturas de su carne, asear, pintar
la mesa y vivir dulcemente
en representación de todo el mundo
y esta cuchara anduvo en su chaqueta,
despierto o bien cuando dormía, siempre,
cuchara muerta viva, ella y sus símbolos.
¡Abisa a todos los compañeros pronto!
¡Viban los compañeros al pie de esta cuchara para siempre!

Lo han matado, obligándole a morir
a Pedro, a Rojas, al obrero, al hombre, a aquél
que nació muy niñín, mirando al cielo,
y que luego creció, se puso rojo
y luchó con sus células, sus nos, sus todavías, sus hambres, sus
                                                    pedazos.

Lo han matado suavemente
entre el cabello de su mujer, la Juana Vázquez,
a la hora del fuego, al año del balazo
y cuando andaba cerca ya de todo.

Pedro Rojas, así, después de muerto,
se levantó, besó su catafalco ensangrentado,
lloró por España
y volvió a escribir con el dedo en el aire:
"¡Viban los compañeros! Pedro Rojas."

Su cadáver estaba lleno de mundo.

Pedro too used to eat
among the creatures of his flesh, to clean up, to paint
the table & to live sweetly
as a representative of everyone,
& this spoon used to be in his jacket,
awake or else when he slept, always,
dead alive spoon, this one & its symbols.
Advise all our combanions quick!
Long live all combanions at the foot of this spoon forever!

He was killed, they forced him to die,
Pedro, Rojas, the worker, the man, the one
who was born a wee little baby, looking at the sky,
& who afterwards grew up, grew red in the face
& fought against his cells, his nos, his yets, his hungers, his
                                                    pieces.

He was killed softly
in his wife's hair, Juana Vázquez by name,
at the hour of fire, in the year of the gunshot,
& when he was already close to everything.

Pedro Rojas, thus, after being dead,
got up, kissed his bloodsmeared casket,
cried for Spain
& again wrote with his finger in the air:
"Long live all combanions. Pedro Rojas."

His corpse was full of world.

IV.

Los mendigos pelean por España,
mendigando en París, en Roma, en Praga
y refrendando así, con mano gótica, rogante,
los pies de los Apóstoles, en Londres, en New York, en México.
Los pordioseros luchan suplicando infernalmente
a Dios por Santander,
la lid en que ya nadie es derrotado.
Al sufrimiento antiguo
danse, encarnízanse en llorar plomo social
al pie del individuo,
y atacan a gemidos, los mendigos,
matando con tan sólo ser mendigos.

Ruegos de infantería,
en que el arma ruega del metal para arriba,
y ruega la ira, más acá de la pólvora iracunda.
Tácitos escuadrones que disparan
con cadencia mortal, su mansedumbre,
desde un umbral, desde sí mismos, ¡ay!, desde sí mismos.
Potenciales guerreros
sin calcetines al calzar el trueno,
satánicos, numéricos,
arrastrando sus títulos de fuerza,
migaja al cinto,

IV.

The beggars fight for Spain,
begging in Paris, in Rome, in Prague
& thus underlining, with an imploring Gothic hand
the feet of the Apostles, in London, in New York, in Mexico.
The beggars are fighting & begging God
satanically for Santander,
that combat in which no longer is anyone defeated.
They deliver themselves to
the old suffering, they insist on crying social lead
at the foot of the individual,
& with moans those beggars attack,
killing by merely being beggars.

Pleas of the infantry
in which the weapon pleads from the metal up
& the wrath pleads, this side of the raging gunpowder.
Silent squadrons which fire,
with mortal cadence, their gentleness
from a threshold, from inside themselves, yes! from inside
themselves.
Potential warriors,
without socks to cannon thunder,
satanic, numerous,
dragging their titles of strength,
crumb under belt,

fusil doble calibre: sangre y sangre.
¡El poeta saluda al sufrimiento armado!

23 de octubre 1937

double caliber rifle: blood & blood.
The poet hails armed suffering!

October 23, 1937

V. Imagen Española de la Muerte

¡Ahí pasa! ¡Llamadla! ¡Es su costado!
Ahí pasa la muerte por Irún:
sus pasos de acordeón, su palabrota,
su metro del tejido que te dije,
su gramo de aquel peso que he callado . . . ¡si son ellos!

¡Llamadla! ¡Daos prisa! Va buscándome en los rifles,
como que sabe bien dónde la venzo,
cuál es mi maña grande, mis leyes especiosas, mis códigos te-
                                                    rribles.
¡Llamadla!, ella camina exactamente como un hombre, entre las
                                                    fieras,
se apoya en aquel brazo que se enlaza a nuestros pies
cuando dormimos en los parapetos
y se pára a las puertas elásticas del sueño.
¡Grito! ¡Grito! ¡Grito su grito nato, sensorial!
Gritara de vergüenza, de ver cómo has caído entre las plantas,
de ver cómo se aleja de las bestias,
de oír cómo decimos: ¡Es la muerte!
¡De herir nuestros más grandes intereses!
(Porque elabora su hígado la gota que te dije, camarada;
porque se come el alma del vecino.)

¡Llamadla! Hay que seguirla
hasta el pie de los tanques enemigos,

V. Spanish Image of Death

There she goes! Call her! It's her side!
There goes Death through Irún:
her accordion steps, her curse,
her meter of the cloth that I've mentioned,
her gram of that weight that I've not mentioned . . . if they're
real!

Call her! Hurry! She seeks me among the rifles,
since she well knows where I defeat her,
what my great trick is, my deceptive laws, my terrible codes.
Call her! she walks exactly like a man, among wild beasts,
she leans on that arm which entwines our feet
when we sleep in the trenches
& she stops at the elastic gates of dream.
She shouted! She shouted! She shouted her born sensorial shout!
She had shouted from shame, from seeing how she's fallen
among the plants,
from seeing how she withdraws from the beasts,
from hearing how we say: It's Death!
From wounding our greatest interests!
(Because her liver manufactures the drop I've mentioned, comrade;
because she eats the soul of our neighbor.)

Call her! We must follow her
to the foot of the enemy tanks,

que la muerte es un sér sido a la fuerza,
cuyo principio y fin llevo grabados
a la cabeza de mis ilusiones,
por mucho que ella corra el peligro corriente que tú
que tú sabes
y que haga como que hace que me ignora.

¡Llamadla! No es un sér, muerte violenta,
sino, apenas, lacónico suceso;
más bien su modo tira, cuando ataca,
tira a tumulto simple, sin órbitas ni cánticos de dicha;
más bien tira su tiempo audaz, a céntimo impreciso
y sus sordos quilates, a déspotas aplausos.
¡Llamadla!, que en llamándola con saña, con figuras,
se la ayuda a arrastrar sus tres rodillas,
como, a veces,
a veces duelen, punzan fracciones enigmáticas, globales,
como, a veces, me palpo y no me siento.

¡Llamadla! ¡Daos prisa! Va buscándome,
con su coñac, su pómulo moral,
sus pasos de acordeón, su palabrota.
¡Llamadla! No hay que perderle el hilo en que la lloro.
De su olor para arriba, ¡ay de mi polvo, camarada!
De su pus para arriba, ¡ay de mi férula, teniente!
De su imán para abajo, ¡ay de mi tumba!

for death is a being been by force,
whose beginning & end I carry engraved
at the head of my illusions,
even though she would run the normal risk that you,
that you know
& though she would pretend to pretend to ignore me.

Call her! Violent death is not a being,
but, hardly, laconic event;
rather her way tends, when she attacks,
tends toward simple tumult, without orbits or joyous songs;
rather her audacious time tends toward imprecise penny
& her deaf carats, toward despotic applause.
Call her! for by calling her with fury, with figures,
you help her drag her three knees,
as, at times,
at times, global enigmatic fractions hurt & pierce,
as, at times, I touch myself & don't feel myself.

Call her! Hurry! She seeks me
with her cognac, her moral cheekbone,
her accordion steps, her curse.
Call her! The thread of my tears for her must not be lost.
From her smell up, Oh God my dust, comrade!
From her pus up, Oh God my ferule, lieutenant!
From her magnet down, Oh God my tomb!

VI. Cortejo tras la Toma de Bilbao

Herido y muerto, hermano,
criatura veraz, republicana, están andando en tu trono,
desde que tu espinazo cayó famosamente;
están andando, pálido, en tu edad flaca y anual,
laboriosamente absorta ante los vientos.

Guerrero en ambos dolores,
siéntate a oír, acuéstate al pie del palo súbito,
inmediato de tu trono;
voltea;
están las nuevas sábanas, extrañas;
están andando, hermano, están andando.

Han dicho: "¡Cómo! ¡Dónde! . . .", expresándose
en trozos de paloma,
y los niños suben sin llorar a tu polvo.
Ernesto Zúñiga, duerme con la mano puesta,
con el concepto puesto,
en descanso tu paz, en paz tu guerra.

Herido mortalmente de vida, camarada,
camarada jinete,
camarada caballo entre hombre y fiera,
tus huesecillos de alto y melancólico dibujo
forman pompa española,
laureada de finísimos andrajos.

VI. Cortege after the Capture
of Bilbao

Wounded & dead, brother,
truthful creature, Loyalist, they are walking on your throne,
ever since your backbone fell famously;
they are walking, pale, on your lean & annual age,
laboriously entranced before the winds.

Warrior in both sorrows,
sit down & listen, lie down at the foot of the sudden stick,
next to your throne;
turn around;
the new sheets are strange;
they are walking, brother, they are walking.

They've said: "How! Where! . . ." speaking
in hunks of dove,
& the children go up to your dust without crying.
Ernesto Zúñiga, sleep with your hand on,
with your concept on,
your peace at rest, your war at peace.

Mortally wounded by life, comrade,
comrade rider,
comrade horse between man & wild beast,
your delicate bones of high & melancholy design
form Spanish pomp
laureled with the finest rags.

Siéntate, pues, Ernesto,
oye que están andando, aquí, en tu trono,
desde que tu tobillo tiene canas.
¿Qué trono?
¡Tu zapato derecho! ¡Tu zapato!

13 de septiembre 1937

Sit down, then, Ernesto,
listen how they are walking, here, on your throne,
ever since your ankle got grey hair.
What throne?
Your right shoe! Your shoe!

September 13, 1937

VII.

Varios días el aire, compañeros,
muchos días el viento cambia de aire,
el terreno, de filo,
de nivel el fusil republicano.
Varios días España está española.

Varios días el mal
moviliza sus órbitas, se abstiene,
paraliza sus ojos escuchándolos.
Varios días orando con sudor desnudo,
los milicianos cuélganse del hombre.
Varios días, el mundo, camaradas,
el mundo está español hasta la muerte.

Varios días ha muerto aquí el disparo
y ha muerto el cuerpo en su papel de espíritu
y el alma es ya nuestra alma, compañeros.
Varios días el cielo,
éste, el del día, el de la pata enorme.

Varios días, Gijón;
muchos dias, Gijón;
mucho tiempo, Gijón;
mucha tierra, Gijón;
mucho hombre, Gijón;
y mucho dios, Gijón,

VII.

For several days the air, companions,
for many days the wind changes air,
the ground, its edge,
its level, the Loyalist rifle.
For several days Spain looks Spanish.

For several days evil
mobilizes its orbits, abstains,
paralyzes its eyes listening to them.
For several days, praying with naked sweat,
the civilian-fighters hang from man.
For several days, the world, comrades,
the world looks Spanish unto death.

For several days the shooting here has died
& the body has died in its spiritual role
& the soul, companions, has become our soul.
For several days the sky,
this sky, the day's, the enormous paw's.

For several days, Gijón;
for many days, Gijón;
for much time, Gijón;
for much land, Gijón;
for much man, Gijón;
& for much God, Gijón,

muchísimas Españas ¡ay!, Gijón.

Camaradas,
varios días el viento cambia de aire.

5 de noviembre 1937

for very many Spains, ale! Gijón.

Comrades,
for several days the wind changes air.

November 5, 1937

VIII.

Aquí,
Ramón Collar,
prosigue tu familia soga a soga,
se sucede,
en tanto, que visitas, tú, allá, a las siete espadas, en Madrid,
en el frente de Madrid.

¡Ramón Collar, yuntero
y soldado hasta yerno de su suegro,
marido, hijo limítrofe del viejo Hijo del Hombre!
Ramón de pena, tú, Collar valiente,
paladín de Madrid y por cojones. ¡Ramonete,
aquí,
los tuyos piensan mucho en tu peinado!

¡Ansiosos, ágiles de llorar, cuando la lágrima!
¡Y cuando los tambores, andan; hablan
delante de tu buey, cuando la tierra!

¡Ramón! ¡Collar! ¡A ti! ¡Si eres herido,
no seas malo en sucumbir; refrénate!
Aquí,
tu cruel capacidad está en cajitas;
aquí,
tu pantalón oscuro, andando el tiempo,
sabe ya andar solísimo, acabarse;

VIII.

Back here,
Ramón Collar,
your family continues from rope to rope,
it goes on,
while you pay a visit, you, out there, to the seven swords, in
                                                    Madrid,
at the front of Madrid.

Ramón Collar, ox-driver
& soldier until son-in-law of his father-in-law,
husband, son bordering the old Son of Man!
Ramón of pain, you, brave Collar,
palatine of Madrid & by sheer balls. Ramonete,
back here,
your people think a lot about your hairdo!

How concerned, quick to cry, when the tear!
And when the drums, they walk; they speak
in front of your ox, when the soil!

Ramón! Collar! To you! If you are wounded,
don't be bad when you succumb; refrain yourself!
Back here,
your cruel capacity is in little boxes;
back here,
your dark trousers, after a while,
already know how to walk in utter solitude, how to wear out;

aquí,
Ramón, tu suegro, el viejo,
te pierde a cada encuentro con su hija!

Te diré que han comido aquí tu carne,
sin saberlo,
tu pecho, sin saberlo,
tu pie;
pero cavilan todos en tus pasos coronados de polvo!

¡Han rezado a Dios,
aquí;
se han sentado en tu cama, hablando a voces
entre tu soledad y tus cositas;
no sé quien ha tomado tu arado, no sé quien
fué a ti, ni quién volvió de tu caballo!
Aquí, Ramón Collar, en fin, tu amigo.
¡Salud, hombre de Dios, mata y escribe!

10 de septiembre 1937

back here,
Ramón, your father-in-law, the old man,
loses you at each encounter with his daughter!

I tell you that back here they've eaten your flesh,
without realizing it,
your chest, without realizing it,
your foot;
but they all brood on your steps crowned with dust!

They've prayed to God,
back here;
they've sat on your bed, talking loudly
among your solitude & your little things;
I don't know who has taken hold of your plow, I don't know
who
went after you, nor who returned from your horse!
Back here, Ramón Collar, at last, your friend:
Hello there, fellow man, kill & write!

September 10, 1937

IX. Pequeño Responso a un Héroe
de la República

Un libro quedó al borde de su cintura muerta,
un libro retoñaba de su cadáver muerto.
Se llevaron al héroe,
y corpórea y aciaga entró su boca en nuestro aliento;
sudamos todos, el ombligo a cuestas;
caminantes las lunas nos seguían;
también sudaba de tristeza el muerto.

Y un libro, en la batalla de Toledo,
un libro, atrás un libro, arriba un libro, retoñaba del cadáver.

Poesía del pómulo morado, entre el decirlo
y el callarlo,
poesía en la carta moral que acompañara
a su corazón.
Quedóse el libro y nada más, que no hay
insectos en la tumba,
y quedó al borde de su manga el aire remojándose
y haciéndose gaseoso, infinito.

Todos sudamos, el ombligo a cuestas,
también sudaba de tristeza el muerto
y un libro, yo lo ví sentidamente,
un libro, atrás un libro, arriba un libro
retoñó del cadáver exabrupto.

10 de septiembre 1937

IX. Short Prayer for a
Dead Loyalist Hero

A book remained at the edge of his dead waist,
a book was sprouting from his dead corpse.
The hero was carried off,
& corporeally & evilly his mouth entered our breath;
all of us sweated, carrying our navels on our shoulders;
wanderers the moons were following us;
the dead man also was sweating from sadness.

And a book, during the battle for Toledo,
a book, a book behind, a book on top, was sprouting from the
                                                        corpse.

Poetry of the purple cheekbone, between saying it
& not saying it,
poetry in the moral map that once accompanied
his heart.
The book remained & nothing else, for there are no
insects in his tomb,
& at the edge of his sleeve the air remained soaking
& becoming gaseous, infinite.

All of us sweated, carrying our navels on our shoulders,
the dead man also was sweating from sadness.
& a book, I saw it sensewise,
a book, a book behind, a book on top
sprouted from the corpse *ex abrupto*.

September 10, 1937

53

X. Invierno en la Batalla de Teruel

¡Cae agua de revólveres lavados!
Precisamente
es la gracia metálica del agua,
en la tarde nocturna en Aragón,
no obstante las construidas yerbas,
las legumbres ardientes, las plantas industriales.

Precisamente,
es la rama serena de la química,
la rama de explosivos en un pelo,
la rama de automóviles en frecuencias y adioses.

Así responde el hombre, así, a la muerte,
así mira de frente y escucha de costado,
así el agua, al contrario de la sangre, es de agua,
así el fuego, al revés de la ceniza, alisa sus rumiantes ateridos.

¿Quién va, bajo la nieve? ¿Están matando? No.
Precisamente,
va la vida coleando, con su segunda soga.
¡Y horrísima es la guerra, solivianta,
lo pone a uno largo, ojoso;
da tumba la guerra, da caer,
da dar un salto extraño de antropoide!
Tú lo hueles, compañero, perfectamente,
al pisar

X. Winter during the Battle for Teruel

Water is dripping from washed revolvers!
It is precisely
the metallic grace of the water,
in the nocturnal afternoon of Aragón,
in spite of the constructed grasses,
the fiery vegetables, the industrial plants.

It is precisely
the serene branch of Chemistry,
the branch of explosives in one hair,
the branch of automobiles in frequencies & goodbyes.

This is how man responds, this is how he responds to death,
this is how he looks forward and listens sideways,
this is how water, contrary to blood, is made of water,
this is how fire, opposite of ash, smooths its ruminant chills.

Who goes there, under the snow? Are they killing? No.
It is precisely
life wagging, with its second rope.
And war is utter horror, it incites,
it makes a man long, all eye,
war creates tomb, creates fall,
creates creating a strange anthropoid jump!
You smell it, perfectly, companion,
on stepping

por distracción tu brazo entre cadáveres;
tú lo ves, pues tocaste tus testículos, poniéndote rojísimo;
tú lo oyes en tu boca de soldado natural.

Vamos, pues, compañero;
nos espera tu sombra apercibida,
nos espera tu sombra acuartelada,
mediodía capitán, noche soldado raso . . .
Por eso, al referirme a esta agonía,
aléjome de mí gritando fuerte:
¡Abajo mi cadáver! . . . Y sollozo.

distractedly on your own arm among the corpses;
you see it, because you touched your testicles, blushing
                                                    intensely;
you hear it in your natural soldier's mouth.

Let's go then, companion;
your alerted shadow waits for us,
your quartered shadow waits for us,
noon captain, night common soldier . . .
That's why, referring to this agony
I withdraw from myself shouting loudly:
Down with my corpse! . . . And I sob.

XI.

Miré el cadáver, su raudo orden visible
y el desorden lentísimo de su alma;
le ví sobrevivir; hubo en su boca
la edad entrecortada de dos bocas.
Le gritaron su número: pedazos.
Le gritaron su amor: ¡más le valiera!
Le gritaron su bala: ¡también muerta!

Y su orden digestivo sosteníase
y el desorden de su alma, atrás, en balde.
Le dejaron y oyeron, y es entonces
que el cadáver
casi vivió en secreto, en un instante;
más le auscultaron mentalmente, ¡y fechas!

3 de septiembre 1937

XI.

I looked at the corpse, at its visible swift order
& at the very slow disorder of its soul;
I saw it survive; there was in its mouth
the faltering age of two mouths.
They shouted its number at it: pieces.
They shouted its love at it: it was not enough!
They shouted its bullet at it: likewise dead!

And its digestive order stood still
& the disorder of its soul, behind, in vain.
They left it & listened, & it is then
that the corpse
almost lived secretly, for an instant;
but they auscultated it mentally—only dates!

September 3, 1937

XII. Masa

Al fin de la batalla,
y muerto el combatiente, vino hacia él un hombre
y le dijo: "¡No mueras; te amo tanto!"
Pero el cadáver ¡ay! siguió muriendo.

Se le acercaron dos y repitiéronle:
"¡No nos dejes! ¡Valor! ¡Vuelve a la vida!"
Pero el cadáver ¡ay! siguió muriendo.

Acudieron a él veinte, cien, mil, quinientos mil,
clamando: "Tánto amor, y no poder nada contra la muerte!"
Pero el cadáver ¡ay! siguió muriendo.

Le rodearon millones de individuos,
con un ruego común: "¡Quédate, hermano!"
Pero el cadáver ¡ay! siguió muriendo.

Entonces todos los hombres de la tierra
le rodearon; les vió el cadáver triste, emocionado;
incorporóse lentamente,
abrazó al primer hombre; echóse a andar . . .

10 de noviembre 1937

XII. Mass

At the end of the battle,
the combatant dead, a man came toward him
& said: "Don't die; I love you so much!"
But oh God the corpse kept on dying.

Two men approached him & repeated:
"Don't leave us! Be brave! Return to life!"
But oh God the corpse kept on dying.

20, 100, 1000, 500,000 came up to him,
exclaiming: "So much love & no power against death!"
But oh God the corpse kept on dying.

Millions of persons surrounded him,
with a common plea: "Stay, brother!"
But oh God the corpse kept on dying.

Then all the inhabitants of the earth
surrounded him; the corpse looked at them sadly, moved:
he sat up slowly,
embraced the first man; began to walk . . .

November 10, 1937

XIII. *Redoble Fúnebre a los Escombros de Durango*

Padre polvo que subes de España,
Dios te salve, libere y corone,
padre polvo que asciendes del alma.

Padre polvo que subes del fuego,
Dios te salve, te calce y dé un trono,
padre polvo que estás en los cielos.

Padre polvo, biznieto del humo,
Dios te salve y ascienda a infinito,
padre polvo, biznieto del humo.

Padre polvo en que acaban los justos,
Dios te salve y devuelva a la tierra,
padre polvo en que acaban los justos.

Padre polvo que creces en palmas,
Dios te salve y revista de pecho,
padre polvo, terror de la nada.

Padre polvo, compuesto de hierro,
Dios te salve y te dé forma de hombre,
padre polvo, que marchas ardiendo.

Padre polvo, sandalia del paria,
Dios te salve y jamás te desate,

XIII. Funereal Drumroll for the
Ruins of Durango

Father dust that rises from Spain,
God save, liberate & crown you,
father dust that ascends from the soul.

Father dust that rises from the fire,
God save you, support you & offer a throne,
father dust who art in heaven.

Father dust, great grandson of the smoke,
God save & raise you to infinity,
father dust, great grandson of the smoke.

Father dust end of the just,
God save & return you to earth,
father dust end of the just.

Father dust that grows into palms,
God save & dress you in chest,
father dust, terror of the void.

Father dust, composed of iron,
God save you & give you human form,
father dust who marches burning.

Father dust, sandal of the pariah,
God save you & never unbind you,

padre polvo, sandalia del paria.

Padre polvo que avientan los bárbaros,
Dios te salve y te ciña de dioses,
padre polvo que escoltan los átomos.

Padre polvo, sudario del pueblo,
Dios te salve del mal para siempre,
padre polvo español, ¡padre nuestro!

Padre polvo que vas al futuro,
Dios te salve, te guie y te dé alas,
padre polvo que vas al futuro.

22 de octubre 1937

father dust, sandal of the pariah.

Father dust fanned by barbarians,
God save you & surround you with gods,
father dust escorted by atoms.

Father dust, shroud of the people,
God save you from evil forever,
Spanish father dust, our father!

Father dust that goes into the future,
God save you, guide you & give you wings,
father dust that goes into the future.

October 22, 1937

XIV. *España, Aparta de mí este Cáliz*

Niños del mundo,
si cae España—digo, es un decir—
si cae
del cielo abajo su antebrazo que asen,
en cabestro, dos láminas terrestres;
niños, ¡qué edad la de las sienes cóncavas!
¡qué temprano en el sol lo que os decía!
¡qué pronto en vuestro pecho el ruido anciano!
¡qué viejo vuestro 2 en el cuaderno!

¡Niños del mundo, está
la madre España con su vientre a cuestas;
está nuestra maestra con sus férulas,
está madre y maestra,
cruz y madera, porque os dió la altura,
vértigo y división y suma, niños;
está con ella, padres procesales!

Si cae—digo, es un decir—si cae
España, de la tierra para abajo,
niños, ¡cómo váis a cesar de crecer!
¡cómo va a castigar el año al mes!
¡cómo van a quedarse en diez los dientes,
en palote el diptongo, la medalla en llanto!
¡Cómo va el corderillo a continuar
atado por la pata al gran tintero!

XIV. *Spain, Take This Cup from Me*

Children of the world,
if Spain falls—I mean, it's just a thought—
if Spain falls
from the sky downward, let her forearm be seized,
in a halter, by two terrestrial plates;
children! what an age the age of the concave temples!
how early in the sun what I was telling you!
how soon in your chest the ancient noise!
how old your 2 in your notebook!

Children of the world,
mother Spain is with her belly on her shoulders;
our teacher is with her ferules,
she is mother & teacher,
cross & wood, because she gave you the height,
dizziness & division & addition, children;
she is with herself, judicial fathers!

If Spain falls—I mean, it's just a thought—if Spain
falls, from the earth downward,
children, how you are going to stop growing!
how the year is going to punish the month!
how you're never going to have more than ten teeth,
how the dipthong will remain in downstroke, the medal in tears!
How the little lamb is going to continue
tied by its leg to the great inkwell!

¡Cómo vais a bajar las gradas del alfabeto
hasta la letra en que nació la pena!

Niños,
hijos de los guerreros, entretanto,
bajad la voz, que España está ahora mismo repartiendo
la energía entre el reino animal,
las florecillas, los cometas y los hombres.
¡Bajad la voz, que está
con su rigor, que es grande, sin saber
qué hacer, y está en su mano
la calavera hablando y habla y habla,
la calavera, aquélla de la trenza,
la calavera, aquélla de la vida!

¡Bajad la voz, os digo;
bajad la voz, el canto de las sílabas, el llanto
de la materia y el rumor menor de las pirámides, y aun
el de las sienes que andan con dos piedras!
¡Bajad el aliento, y si
el antebrazo baja,
si las férulas suenan, si es la noche,
si el cielo cabe en dos limbos terrestres,
si hay ruido en el sonido de las puertas,
si tardo,
si no véis a nadie, si os asustan
los lápices sin punta, si la madre
España cae—digo, es un decir—
salid, niños del mundo; id a buscarla! . . .

How you are going to descend the steps of the alphabet
to the letter in which pain was born!

Children,
sons of warriors, meanwhile,
lower your voice, for Spain is right this moment distributing
her energy among the animal kingdom,
little flowers, comets & men.
Lower your voice, for she is
with her rigor, which is great, not knowing
what to do, & she has in her hand
the skull talking & it talks & talks,
the skull, with the braid,
the skull, that is alive!

Lower your voice, I tell you;
lower your voice, the song of syllables, the crying
of matter & the lesser rumor of pyramids, & even
that of the temples which walk with two stones!
Lower your breathing, & if
the forearm lowers,
if the ferules sound, if it is night,
if heaven fits in two terrestrial limbos,
if there's noise in the sound of the doors,
if I am late,
if you don't see anyone, if the unsharpened pencils
frighten you, if mother
Spain falls—I mean, it's just a thought—
Out, children of the world, go & look for her! . . .

XV.

¡Cuídate, España, de tu propia España!
¡Cuídate de la hoz sin el martillo!
¡Cuídate del martillo sin la hoz!
¡Cuídate de la víctima a pesar suyo,
del verdugo a pesar suyo
y del indiferente a pesar suyo!
¡Cuídate del que, antes de que cante el gallo,
negárate tres veces,
y del que te negó, después, tres veces!
¡Cuídate de las calaveras sin las tibias,
y de las tibias sin las calaveras!
¡Cuídate de los nuevos poderosos!
¡Cuídate del que come tus cadáveres,
del que devora muertos a tus vivos!
¡Cuídate del leal ciento por ciento!
¡Cuídate del cielo más acá del aire
y cuídate del aire más allá del cielo!
¡Cuídate de los que te aman!
¡Cuídate de tus héroes!
¡Cuídate de tus muertos!
¡Cuídate de la República!
¡Cuídate del futuro! . . .

10 de octubre 1937

XV.

Beware, Spain, of your own Spain!
Beware of the sickle without the hammer!
Beware of the hammer without the sickle!
Beware of the victim in spite of himself,
of the hangman in spite of himself
& of the uncommitted in spite of himself!
Beware of the one who, before the cock crows,
will have denied you three times,
& of the one who denied you, afterwards, three times!
Beware of the skulls without tibias,
& of the tibias without skulls!
Beware of the new potentates!
Beware of the one who eats your corpses,
of the one who devours dead your living!
Beware of the one hundred percent loyal!
Beware of the sky this side of air
& beware of the air beyond the sky!
Beware of those who love you!
Beware of your heros!
Beware of your dead!
Beware of the Republic!
Beware of the future! . . .

October 10, 1937

Notes

Nine of these poems appear to have been written between September and November of 1937. However, since Vallejo apparently would date a poem after making final revisions, dates do not necessarily mean a poem was completely written on the dated day or even at the time (the poet's widow, for example, states that "Mass" was written in 1929). Six of these poems have no dates, and at least one of them, "Winter During the Battle for Teruel," must have been written after the September-November composition period because the battle for Teruel did not take place until the end of 1937, continuing to February 22, 1938. Some of the composition mystery may relate to problems concerning the original publication of the book: the first edition was printed by Loyalist soldiers on paper they themselves had made and was on the verge of being published when Catalonia fell; the entire first edition was thus destroyed, presumably by the victorious Fascist troops. Catalonia fell in January 1939; Vallejo had died in Paris in April 1938. In 1940 a first edition was published in Mexico by Editorial Séneca, with an introduction by Juan Larrea, which has served as the text for all subsequent editions. We do not know if the Séneca edition is identical to the manuscript Vallejo gave to the Loyalist soldiers. Since at the present time there is no way to check this out, our translation is based on the Séneca edition and follows its poem order. While Vallejo was composing/revising the present book he was also composing/revising many other poems posthumously published as *Poemas Humanos*. In a way, the present collection of 15 poems is a part of the 93-poem *Poemas Humanos* and it is very interesting to read the dated poems of both volumes chronologically. Such a reading reveals that the Spanish Civil War was but an aspect of man's fate which preoccupied Vallejo at that time. For biographical material on Vallejo's years in Europe the reader is referred to the introduction in *Poemas Humanos/Human Poems*, translated by Clayton Eshleman and published by Grove Press, New York City, 1968.

I   Hymn to The Volunteers for the Republic

Line 1: "miliciano" is literally "militiaman." Because of current American connotations of this word we have decided that "civilian-fighter" conveys more accurately the meaning that "miliciano" acquired during the Spanish Civil War.

Line 8: "pecho" is literally "chest," and while the word is a little awkward in English we have decided to stick with it because although its interpretation would be "heart" or "courage," Vallejo uses the word often, giving it a feeling of his own. In Spanish there is an idiomatic expression, "dar el pecho"—"to show courage"— e.g., "Ir al frente y dar el pecho."

Line 9: we have used a neologism here to get at the particular edge of Vallejo's "desgraciarme." "Degrace" is to function like "delouse"—the idea being to divest oneself of grace. The expression could also mean "disgrace myself" or "feel miserable."

Lines 19–21: here Vallejo fully opens himself to the conflict, & thus to death, envisioning this act as a torero working against a bull's "double-edged speed." His "costumed in greatness" is the bullfighter's garb, his "traje de luces."

Line 23: the biennial referred to here is the period 1934–36 called "el bienio negro"—"the black biennial" which preceded the war.

Line 42: Pedro Calderón de la Barca (1600–1681), famous Spanish playwright, author of *Life Is A Dream*. Lines 42 through 52 are an extraordinary weave of great Spanish figures of the past and contemporary heroes.

Line 47: Antonio Coll, popular hero during the war. He was the first to, on foot, knock out Italian tanks with homemade hand grenades.

Line 49: Francisco de Quevedo (1580–1645), famous satirist, perhaps the Spanish poet most admired by Vallejo.

Line 50: Santiago Ramón y Cajal (1852–1934), famous histologist who shared in the Nobel Prize for medicine in 1906. He specialized in the microscopic study of cells in the nervous system.

Line 51: Teresa de Jesus (1515–1582), famous mystic and writer, to whom is attributed the sonnet which begins "I die because I am not dying."

Line 52: Lina Odena, popular heroine who died fighting Fascism on the southern front.

Line 121: an allusion to the Abyssinian "negus" or "lion of Judea" exiled by the invading Mussolini forces. The Italians fought on both sides during the Spanish Civil War.

Line 130: "ferula," like "pecho," is a word that seems to have had a special significance for Vallejo, so again we have not interpreted it. He uses it several times in the book, each time with a slightly different connotation. Here it appears to imply the source of one's discipline.

II

Line 1: Estremadura is the western region of Spain known for its poverty and absentee landowners. The first important battle of the war took place here. Estremadura was finally overrun by colonial Moorish troops brought to Spain to fight for the Fascist rebels.

Line 43: Talavera de la Reina, a town in the province of Toledo taken by Fascist troops on September 5, 1936, on their way toward Madrid.

Line 60: Guernica, immortalized in the famous painting by Picasso, was the sacred town of the Basque people of northern Spain. German bombers, authorized by Franco, destroyed it completely on April 26, 1937, even though it had no military value.

Line 94: Málaga was taken by the Italian General Roatta's troops on February 8, 1937. Thousands of the city's inhabitants fled along the coast toward Almería and were killed in great numbers by German naval fire and German and Italian bombers.

III

Line 2: Pedro Rojas appears to be a fictitious character, a symbol of the most humble and oppressed human beings. He has just learned to write a little, and hearing "avisa" as "abisa" misspells the word. We pick up the misspelling in "combanions" for "companions."

IV

Line 18: the Spanish "ay!" is an exclamation that conveys sorrow, lament, or pain. Vallejo uses the cry in several differing contexts in these poems, and we have rendered it a little differently on each occasion, attempting to capture the spontaneous thrust of emotion.

Line 20: "sin calcetines al calzar el trueno" does not have an equivalent in English. "Calzar un cañon" means "to load a cannon." The word "calcetines" means "socks," having lost its meaning as a diminutive of "calza"; "sin calcetines" can be translated as "barefoot" or "without socks." "Calza" could also mean "wedge" or "support."

V Spanish Image of Death

Line 2: Irún, a Basque town very close to the French-Spanish border, occupied by Fascist troops on September 5, 1936, after being ferociously attacked by sea, air, and land.

VI Cortege after the Capture of Bilbao

Title: Bilbao, the greatest industrial city in northern Basque Spain, fell into Fascist hands on July 18, 1937.

Line 2: to translate "republicana" here as "Republican" would be misleading. "Loyalist" conveys the idea of one loyal to the existing government, the Spanish Republic.

VII

Line 18: Gijón, industrial town in the northern province of Asturias, which withstood Fascist attack for a long time before being evacuated on October 21, 1937.

VIII

Line 2: Ramón Collar (pronounced Ko-yar), probably a fictitious name, symbolizing a peasant-soldier in the defense of Madrid.

X Winter during the Battle for Teruel

Title: the battle for Teruel took place in terrible
weather (the temperature got as low as 20 degrees be-
low zero) from December 15, 1937, to February 22,
1938. It was perhaps the most ferocious battle of the
war.

XIII Funereal Drumroll for the Ruins of Durango

Title: Durango, a town in the Basque province of
Viscaya that was destroyed by repeated German air
raids, at almost the same time Guernica was, April 26,
1937.

XIV Spain, Take This Cup from Me

Title: Jesus at Gethsemane: "My Father, if it be pos-
sible, let this cup pass away from me: nevertheless, not
as I will, but as thou wilt." Matthew 26:39. We have
not felt bound to copy the Biblical version of the
phrase, but have rendered it more actively.

Lines 6 and 41: "sienes," "temples," refer only to the
human head.

—Clayton Eshleman and
José Rubia Barcia
Los Angeles,
1973